Around the World

Food

Margaret Hall

Heinemann
LIBRARY

H www.heinemann/library.co.uk
Visit our website to find out more information about Heinemann Library books.

To order:
☎ Phone 44 (0) 1865 888066
📄 Send a fax to 44 (0) 1865 314091
💻 Visit the Heinemann Library Bookshop at www.heinemann/library.co.uk to browse our catalogue and order online.

First published in Great Britain by Heinemann Library, Halley Court, Jordan Hill, Oxford OX2 8EJ, a division of Reed Educational and Professional Publishing Ltd. Heinemann is a registered trademark of Reed Educational and Professional Publishing Ltd.

OXFORD MELBOURNE AUCKLAND JOHANNESBURG BLANTYRE
GABORONE IBADAN PORTSMOUTH (NH) USA CHICAGO

© Reed Educational and Professional Publishing Ltd 2002
The moral right of the proprietor has been asserted.

Designed by Lisa Buckley
Originated by Dot Gradations
Printed in Hong Kong/China

ISBN 0 431 15121 0 (hardback)   ISBN 0 431 15126 1 (paperback)
06 05 04 03 02   07 06 05 04 03 02
10 9 8 7 6 5 4 3 2   10 9 8 7 6 5 4 3 2 1

British Library Cataloguing in Publication Data
Hall, Margaret
   Food. - (Around the world)
   1.Food - Juvenile literature
   I.Title
   641.3

Acknowledgements
The publishers would like to thank the following for permission to reproduce photographs: Robert Frerck/Tony Stone, p., 1, 11; Wolfgang Kaehler, pp.4a, 17, 21; Keren Su/Tony Stone, p., 4b; Sharon Smith/Bruce Coleman, Inc., p. 4c; Anna E. Zuckermann/Photo Edit, p. 5; Fulvio Eccardi/ECCAR/Bruce Coleman, Inc., p. 6; Wayne Estep/Tony Stone, p. 7; David Hiser/Tony Stone, p. 8; James Nelson/Tony Stone, p. 9; Bob Krist/Corbis, p. 10; Mike Price/Bruce Coleman, Inc., p. 12; Penny Tweedie/Corbis, p. 13; Paul Conklin/Photo Edit, p. 14; Bios (Klein & Hubert)/Peter Arnold, p. 15; Scott Camazine/Photo Researchers, p. 16; Galen Rowell/Corbis, p. 18; Art Wolfe/Tony Stone, p. 19; Jeff Greenberg/Photo Edit, p. 20; Bryan Mullennix/MULLE/Bruce Coleman, Inc., p. 22; Jeff Greenbert/Peter Arnold, p. 23; Holt Studios/Photo Researcher, p. 24; Carl Purcell/Photo Researchers, p. 25; Tom Stewart/The Stock Market, p. 26; Richard Hutchings/Photo Researchers, p. 27; Ric Ergenbright, p. 28; Tony Freeman/Photo Edit, p. 29.

Cover photograph reproduced with permission of Fulvio Eccardi/ECCAR/Bruce Coleman, Inc.

Every effort has been made to contact copyright holders of any material reproduced in this book. Any omissions will be rectified in subsequent printings if notice is given to the publishers.

Any words appearing in the text in bold, **like this**, are explained in the glossary.

Contents

People have needs 4

People need food 6

Getting food 8

Food around the world 10

Growing food 12

Finding food 14

Keeping animals for food 16

Food from the water 18

Food in tropical places 20

Food in temperate places 22

Food in cold places 24

Special food 26

Food on the move .28

Photo list 30

Glossary 31

More books to read 32

Index 32

People have needs

People everywhere have the same **needs**. They need water, clothing, homes and **transport**. All around the world, people also need food.

Some food may be the same in different parts of the world. Some food may be different.

People need food

No one can live without food. Food gives people **energy** and makes their bodies grow. Eating the right kinds of food keeps people healthy.

There are other reasons for eating, too. People share food to show that they are friends. They eat together to **celebrate** special days.

Getting food

What people eat depends on the **climate** in the place where they live. It also depends on what they can grow, catch or buy to eat.

Some people grow, **gather** or hunt their own food. Other people get all the food they eat from shops or markets.

Food around the world

Food **customs** in one place may seem strange in another. Some people might eat raw fish. They might think that eating butter and cheese is strange.

Even a food found all around the world is not always the same. Bread in one part of the world might not look or taste like the bread somewhere else!

Growing food

People grow many kinds of **crops** for food. Soya beans are grown and used to make different kinds of food and drinks.

People also grow fruits and vegetables to eat. Which ones they grow depend on the **climate** in the place where they live.

Finding food

In some places, people get most of their food from the land around them. They may grow some of the food they eat. They need to make sure there is enough water for their plants.

People also pick wild foods such as berries and mushrooms. They may hunt animals and catch fish to eat.

Keeping animals for food

People also keep animals that are used for food. Some people keep animals for the milk or eggs they give.

Other animals are kept for their meat.
Many people eat the meat of animals like
cows, pigs, sheep and chickens.

Food from the water

Many fish and other animals live in oceans, lakes and rivers. People who live near water eat a lot of these fish and animals. They also eat water plants, such as seaweed.

The kind of fish people eat also depends on where they live. Some fish are caught in warm water. Other fish, like salmon and cod, live in cooler water.

Food in tropical places

Tropical places are hot and wet. Many fruits and vegetables grow well in tropical **climates**. Fruits like bananas and pineapples grow only in tropical places.

Tropical climates are also good for **crops** that need lots of water, such as rice. In tropical climates, food grows all the year round.

Food in temperate places

Temperate climates are warm in summer and cold in winter. **Grains** such as wheat and barley grow well in these places. So do fruits and vegetables such as apples and peas.

Crops do not grow outside during the winter. People may buy food grown in warmer places. Some food is saved to eat during the cold weather.

Food in cold places

In a cold **climate**, the **growing season** is very short. Many plants people eat can only be grown in **greenhouses**. It is warmer in greenhouses than it is outside.

Root vegetables, such as potatoes and carrots, only need a short growing season. These vegetables keep for a long time.

Special food

People eat special foods to **celebrate festivals** or special days. In some places, people roast a whole pig or goat. In other places, there might be special cakes or puddings.

Many people eat special foods because of their **religion**. They may sometimes eat a special meal. Some people never eat certain foods because of what they believe.

Food on the move

Food is often sent from where it is grown and sold to people far away. It is moved in lorries, trains, ships and planes.

Large **supermarkets** sell foods from all over the world. A fruit grown in a **temperate** climate might be eaten by someone who lives in a **tropical** country.

Photo list

Page 4   Food from Saudi Arabia; three generations of a family in Anhui, China; camel pulling a wagon in Jaipur, India

Page 5   Chopping coconuts in Kapingamarangi Island, Micronesia

Page 6   Market in Kampala, Uganda

Page 7   Men sharing a meal in a tent in Saudi Arabia

Page 8   Inuit man fishing, Hudson Bay, Canada

Page 9   Market in Chichicastenango, Guatemala

Page 10   Japanese meal

Page 11   Boy with bread in Anatolia, Turkey

Page 12   Soya bean fields in Maryland, USA

Page 13   Watering banana plants in northern Australia

Page 14   Collecting water for a garden in Chansha, China

Page 15   Picking wild bilberries in France

Page 17   Boy herding cattle in the Maasai Mara, Kenya

Page 18   Off the coast of Newfoundland, Canada

Page 19   Salmon in the Umatilla River, Oregon, USA

Page 20   Harvesting pineapples in Lanai, Hawaii, USA

Page 21   Planting rice near Haiphong, North Vietnam

Page 22   Apple orchard in the Willamette Valley, Oregon, USA

Page 24   Greenhouse in Andalucia, Spain

Page 25   Market in Helsinki, Finland

Page 27   Jewish family celebrating the Sedar festival

Page 28   Banana lorry in Ecuador

Glossary

celebrate do something special for an event or holiday. There may be a party.

climate weather in an area throughout the year

crop plant grown for food

custom way something has been done for a long time

energy ability to move about and be active

festival time of celebration, usually with special events

gather pick and collect food growing in the wild

grain plant that produces seeds or kernels used as food, such as rice, oats, wheat or barley

greenhouse building where plants can be grown in cold weather

growing season time when the weather is warm enough for plants to grow

needs things people must have in order to live

religion what a person believes about God

root vegetable plant with roots that are eaten, such as potatoes, carrots, turnips or radishes

supermarket large food store

temperate having warm summers and cool or cold winters

transport ways people move from place to place

tropical hot and rainy

More books to read

Bread by Louise Spilsbury, Heinemann Library, 2001

Eggs by Louise Spilsbury, Heinemann Library, 2001

Food by Godfrey Hall, Hodder Wayland, 1999

Jody's Beans by Malachy Doyle, Walker, 2000

Potatoes by Louise Spilsbury, Heinemann Library, 2001

Rice by Louise Spilsbury, Heinemann Library, 2001

Rosie Plants a Radish by Kate Petty, Macmillan Children's
  Books, 1997

Index

bread 11

climate 8, 13

   cold 24–25

   temperate 22–23, 29

   tropical 20–21, 29

crops 12, 21, 23

energy 6

fish 10, 15, 18–19

fruit 13, 20, 22, 29

grains 22

greenhouses 24

growing season 24–25

hunting 9, 15

meat 17

needs 4

religion 27

soya beans 12

supermarkets 29

vegetables 13, 20, 22, 25